Table of Contents

My Science Notebook

Dinosaurs

By Martine Podesto

Please visit our web site at **www.garethstevens.com**.
For a free catalog describing Gareth Stevens Publishing's list of high-quality books,
call 1-800-542-2595 (USA) or 1-800-387-3178 (Canada).
Gareth Stevens Publishing's fax: 1-877-542-2596

Library of Congress Cataloging-in-Publication Data
Podesto, Martine.
    Dinosaurs/by Martine Podesto.
        p. cm.—(My Science Notebook)
    Includes bibliographical references and index.
    ISBN-10: 0-8368-9213-5 (lib. bdg.)
    ISBN-13: 978-0-8368-9213-0 (lib. bdg.)
    1. Dinosaurs—Juvenile literature. I. Title.
QE861.5.P635   2008
567.9—dc22   2008012427

This North American edition first published in 2009 by
Gareth Stevens Publishing
A Weekly Reader® Company
1 Reader's Digest Rd.
Pleasantville, NY 10570-7000 USA

This edition copyright © 2009 by Gareth Stevens, Inc. Original edition copyright © 2007 by
QA International., First published in Canada by QA International, Montreal, Quebec.

Gareth Stevens Senior Managing Editor: Lisa M. Herrington
Gareth Stevens Creative Director: Lisa Donovan
Gareth Stevens Senior Designer: Keith Plechaty
Gareth Stevens Associate Editor: Amanda Hudson

Photo Credits:
p. 8: Universitat de les Illes Balears; p. 39: Roger Weller; p. 42: Matthew Hayward;
p. 73: John Adamek, EDCOPE Enterprises; p. 83: Keijo Karvonen; p. 85: Dave Dyet.

Printed in the United States of America

1 2 3 4 5 6 7 8 9 10 09 08

My Science Notebook
Dinosaurs

By Martine Podesto

Science and Curriculum Consultant:
Debra Voege, M.A., Science Curriculum Reso

Gareth Stevens
Publishing

Dear Reader,

Have you ever been frightened by *Tyrannosaurus's* powerful jaws, or fascinated by *Diplodocus's* towering height? Ever since their discovery, **dinosaurs** have amazed us.

I invite you to explore their world, filled with stories of creatures now extinct. When did the dinosaurs appear? What color were they? How did they disappear? These are just some of the questions sent to me by curious readers like you.

Over the years, I've collected so many questions that I decided to answer them in this notebook. I've pasted in some photos and drawings, and drawn some simple diagrams. I hope you enjoy your journey into this world.

Happy reading!

Professor Brainy

Deinonychus

Dear Professor Brainy,

I went to visit the American Museum of Natural History with my class. The dinosaur fossils were great! Our teacher told us that these giant reptiles lived a long time ago. Can you tell me exactly when dinosaurs appeared?

Quentin, age 9

Dear Quentin,

When I was your age, I spent my summer vacations in New York City. My grandparents lived right near the American Museum of Natural History. I often went there on Saturday afternoons to look at the dinosaur skeletons. Just like you, I was fascinated by these amazing **prehistoric** creatures. To get back to your question, dinosaurs appeared about 230 million years ago. They were on Earth for a little more than 164 million years. If you know your math, this means that they vanished about

66 million years ago. (Humans have been on Earth "only" about 5 million years!)

Such long periods of time can be difficult for us to picture. To help us see how time has passed, scientists have found it useful to show the history of the Earth as if it were a single day. Here is what that day looks like: Earth forms at midnight, the start of the day.

Midnight 12:00

Earth appears
(4,600 million years ago)

10:07 a.m.

First amphibians
(360 million
years ago)

9:31 a.m.

First fish
(475 million years ago)

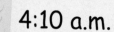

4:10 a.m.

First bacteria
(3,800 million years ago)

The first living cells appear around 4:10 a.m. They look a lot like the bacteria we know today. Life continues to appear, mainly in the oceans, until about 10:20 p.m. At 10:48 p.m., dinosaurs make their appearance. They disappear 51 minutes later, at 11:39 p.m.! Finally, human beings appear at 11:59 p.m., just one minute before the end of the day!

10:49 p.m.

First mammals
(225 million years ago)

11:12 p.m.

First birds
(150 million years ago)

10:48 p.m.

First dinosaurs
(230 million years ago)

10:21 p.m.

First reptiles
(315 million years ago)

11:59 p.m.

Humans appear
(5 million years ago)

Good question, Latifa!

At the time of dinosaurs, Earth looked nothing like the planet we know today. Dinosaurs lived during a time called the **Mesozoic Era**. This era is divided into three shorter periods: the **Triassic**, the **Jurassic**, and the **Cretaceous**.

Ginkgo leaves

Dinosaurs first appeared during the Triassic Period. Back then, Earth was one huge continent, called **Pangaea**. The climate was hot and humid. Giant ferns, conifers, ginkgos, and horsetails grew near the coasts. The land in the middle of the continent was desert. Reptiles ruled the Triassic Period! They were everywhere—in the air, in the water, and on land, where they lived alongside small mammals.

Horsetail

Birds first appeared in the skies during the Jurassic Period. Pangaea began to separate into several pieces. These pieces eventually became the continents we know today. The climate was still hot and humid, and there were many **coniferous** forests.

During the Cretaceous Period, the continents continued to move farther apart. Flowering plants, such as rosebushes, and leafy trees, like oaks and maples, appeared during this period. Pollinating insects—bees, wasps, and butterflies—also appeared, and carried pollen from flower to flower. The dinosaurs disappeared at the end of the Cretaceous, leaving room for many other kinds of animals!

Yours truly,
Professor Brainy

Hello Gregory,

As I wrote to Latifa, the period when the
dinosaurs first appeared, the Triassic, was
also the golden age of reptiles! There were
several important groups of primitive, or
ancient, reptiles. *Saurosuchus* weighed 2 tons
and ate just about every other kind of animal.
Euparkeria, a very thin-bodied reptile, looked
a little like today's crocodile. *Lystrosaurus*
was an odd-looking **herbivore**, or plant eater.
It had two large teeth, and a beak for cutting
and tearing leaves. Other reptiles, like the

Saurosuchus

pterosaur, leaped from
treetops and sailed
through the air on
wing-like flaps of
skin. Reptiles also
lived in the oceans.

Pterosaur

The ichthyosaur, for example, looked
like a dolphin, but measured up to 48 feet
(15 m) in length! So as you can see, Gregory,
the dinosaurs would have met up with all these
different animals. It didn't take much time,
however, for the dinosaurs to increase their
numbers and take over the planet!

Best regards,
Professor Brainy

Shonisaurus

Dear Professor Brainy,

How do scientists study dinosaurs?

Thank you.

Ming, age 10

Dear Ming,

The scientists you are talking about are called **paleontologists**. They study dinosaurs the same way detectives investigate a case. The clues they look for are called **fossils**. Fossils are the remains of living things from the past. Dinosaur fossils usually consist of bones, teeth, or footprints.

To find fossils, paleontologists search in mountains and along riverbanks for an area that contains **sedimentary rock**. This rock is made up of leftover pieces from other rocks and the remains of plants and animals that have piled up over the years. Sedimentary rock often contains fossils. Sometimes a fossil is only partly buried in the ground or may come loose from the rock that surrounds it. All the paleontologist has to do is bend down to pick it up! At other times, a fossil may be wedged into a rock. The paleontologist then uses a hammer to break the rock and a brush to gently dust off the fossil.

There is one more important thing for our "detective" to find out: the fossil's age. There are several ways to do this. One method is to figure out the age of the rock itself.

Pick

Ruler

Notebook

In general, rocks that lie deeper
in the ground are older than rocks
that lie closer to the surface. When
paleontologists find fossils in the
ground, they need to know how old
the ground is. That will tell them
how old the fossil is.

Paleontologists have to be very patient.
A team of paleontologists may spend
many years uncovering one dinosaur
skeleton! Who knows? Maybe one
day, Ming, you too will help
dig out a dinosaur.

Brush

Take care,
Professor Brainy

Gloves

Hello Professor Brainy,

Do we know all the dinosaurs that ever lived on Earth?

Thanks.

Thomas, age 11

Hello Thomas,

Discoveries by paleontologists have made it possible to identify almost 800 **species** of dinosaur. But some experts think that there could have been 500,000 species of dinosaur. That's 600 times more than what has been discovered to date!

Did you know that scientists describe a new species based on the fossils they find? The fossils could be a complete or partial skeleton, or even just a bone or a tooth! The formation of fossils is quite rare. For an animal to fossilize, it must be buried quickly after it dies. It might be covered in mud, fine sand, or volcanic ash. Let's imagine a small dinosaur that has been wounded after a fight. It heads for a lake in search of water. Unfortunately, its wounds are serious and it dies shortly afterward. Its body is quickly buried by the mud and decomposes at the bottom of the lake. Now, take a look at the illustrations below. They give you an idea of how the

How a Mollusk Becomes a Fossil

1. The mollusk settles at the lake or sea bottom. Its shell, which is very hard, is preserved.

2. The shell is covered in fine sand and pebbles that are transformed into sedimentary rock. The shell is trapped in this rock.

dinosaur, just like this **mollusk**, turns into a fossil.

If paleontologists have found only 800 species of dinosaur so far, it is because very few dinosaurs were ever fossilized. Also, a lot of Earth that is likely to contain fossils has not yet come up to the surface.

3. Millions of years pass until this rock is brought to the surface by movements in Earth's crust. The shell may then be found by a paleontologist.

You see, Thomas, we don't know ALL the dinosaurs that ever lived on Earth. It's nice to think, though, that many wonderful surprises are still waiting to be discovered!

Your friend,
Professor Brainy

Dear Professor Brainy,

In one of the books I read, one dinosaur is called *Brontosaurus*. A drawing of the same dinosaur in another book is called *Apatosaurus*. Is it a mistake?

Thanks,

Laurie, age 10

Dear Laurie,

Congratulations! You've found an example of mistaken identity. It's the story of a scientist who discovered one new dinosaur, but thought he had discovered two. In 1877, Professor O.C. Marsh discovered a fossil of a dinosaur that looked like *Diplodocus*. In fact, the dinosaur he found wasn't the famous long-necked plant-eater. It was a new species that he called *Apatosaurus*, which means "deceptive lizard."

Two years later, Professor Marsh thought he had found a second species of dinosaur. He called it *Brontosaurus*. In 1903, however, another scientist studying these precious fossils realized that all the bones actually belonged to the same species—*Apatosaurus!* What does one do in a case like this? Well, we always keep the first name that is given—that's the rule! In this case, our good old dinosaur inherited the name *Apatosaurus*. In other books today, though, we still see the name *Brontosaurus*. Can you guess why? Well, it's simply because the authors didn't know everything that we know!

Apatosaurus

One thing is certain: *Apatosaurus*, the "deceptive lizard," ended up with a name that perfectly suits its story!

Your friend,
Professor Brainy

Brontosaurus

Dear Professor,
What did
dinosaurs eat?
Thanks,
Gabriel, age 9

Hello Gabriel,

When I was your age, I collected model
dinosaurs. When I played with them, I would
put them into two groups. Then I would make
them eat each other after a long fight! We
often imagine that all dinosaurs were ferocious
meat eaters. Some were, it's true, but not
all. Let's take a closer look. The shape of the
teeth and the jaws tells us what dinosaurs ate.

Paleontologists found that some dinosaurs ate only plants. They were called herbivores. These included long-necked dinosaurs like *Diplodocus*. This dinosaur had teeth that were tall, slim, and pencil-like. It used them like the prongs on a rake to tear leaves from the trees. The *Diplodocus's* teeth and jaws did not allow it to chew, so it swallowed the leaves right away. Other herbivores had flat teeth at the back of their jaws that allowed them to chew up leaves.

Diplodocus skull

Dinosaurs that ate meat, fish, or insects were **carnivores**. This group includes the large and terrifying *Tyrannosaurus*. It had a powerful set of jaws and teeth sharpened like steak knives. The slightly curved shape of the teeth helped *Tyrannosaurus* hold onto its meal. There was a third group of dinosaurs that ate a little of everything, the same way we do! They were **omnivores**. *Pelecanimimus*, for example, had a beak lined with about 220 tiny and very pointed teeth. These teeth allowed it to eat meat as well as cut up

Tyrannosaurus skull

leaves. Paleontologists have discovered
dinosaur food by examining nearby
fossils. Sometimes they find
a dinosaur skeleton
along with a meal
the dinosaur
swallowed just
before it died.

Pelecanimimus skull

They may also find
fossilized droppings that contain the remains
of a meal. By studying these closely, they learn
more about what the dinosaurs ate.

Regards,
Professor Brainy

Dear Professor,

My cousin told me that plants and animals are grouped into families. Is that true for the dinosaurs, too?

Thanks very much.
Kareem, age 11

Hello Kareem, and hello to your cousin, too!

At the start of each year, I put all my papers in order. I sort through my newspaper clippings, my magazine articles, and everything that is scattered across my desk. Putting all these papers into groups helps me find the information later and use it more easily. For the same reasons, scientists sort things into categories, too, including all the plants and animals. Your cousin is right! Plants and animals are grouped into families. The cat, for example, belongs to the Felidae family, just like the panther and the leopard. Dinosaurs belong to a different family, Dinosauria. These animals are classified in two different groups according to the shape of their pelvis. (The pelvis is the part of the skeleton that connects the spinal column to the hind legs.) And so, there is a group of dinosaurs called the **Saurischians**. Their pelvis looks like that of a lizard. Another group of dinosaurs is called the **Ornithischians**. Their pelvis looks like the pelvis of a bird. I've drawn a diagram for you on the next page. It will help you to understand what comes next.

Carnivores like
Tyrannosaurus

Saurischians

Herbivores like
Diplodocus

Among the
Saurischians, we
find carnivores that
walked on two legs, like *Tyrannosaurus*.
We also find herbivores that walked
on all four legs, such as *Diplodocus*. In
the group of *Ornithischians*, however, we
only find herbivores. Some, like *Triceratops*,
Ankylosaurus, and *Stegosaurus*, walked on all
fours. Others, like *Pachycephalosaurus* and

Horned dinosaurs like *Triceratops*

Armored dinosaurs like *Ankylosaurus*

Plated dinosaurs like *Stegosaurus*

Ornithischians

Dome-headed dinosaurs like *Pachycephalosaurus*

Duck-billed dinosaurs like *Parasaurolophus*

Dinosaurs

Parasaurolophus, could walk on their hind legs.

I hope this answers your question, Kareem!

Professor Brainy

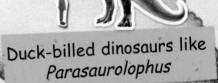

33

Dear Professor Brainy,

Did dinosaurs waddle like lizards or drag themselves along the ground like crocodiles?

Thanks for your answer.
Melanie, age 10

Dear Melanie,

I used to go to the zoo when I was a kid. I watched the crocodiles and wondered if they were bothered by their big stomach, which almost touched the ground when they walked. Dinosaurs were different from crocodiles, though. Their midsection, or abdomen, did not drag along the ground. Do you know why, Melanie? On crocodiles and other reptiles, the legs are set on the sides of the body, and never completely straighten. When the animal walks, it has to do "push-ups." Imagine how difficult it would be to perform this "exercise" with every step you take! That's what crocodiles do. Dinosaurs, however, had legs positioned directly under their body, the same way birds and mammals do. In this position, the dinosaur's weight was supported by a set of legs it could straighten. Without the need to push up its body weight with each step, the dinosaur did not use up all its energy when it walked. This left dinosaurs with energy for other things, like growing tall, running, and supporting a very long neck.

Take care,

Professor Brainy

Hello Professor Brainy,
I heard that some dinosaurs had a kind of bird beak. What was it used for?
Yasmina, age 9

Dear Yasmina,

Corythosaurus used its beak to tear leaves and pinecones off trees. It chewed this meal using the many teeth at the back of its jaws. Another duck-billed dinosaur, called *Edmontosaurus*, had almost 2,000 teeth at the back of its beak! These tiny teeth worked like a cheese grater, cutting and grinding up the plants the dinosaur had been grazing on. Have you noticed a beak on any other dinosaurs?

Corythosaurus skull

Triceratops had a specially hooked beak. It helped the dinosaur tear through tough leaves and hard stalks, allowing it to eat almost any vegetation. The animal then ground the vegetation with its many rows of teeth at the back of its jaws. *Oviraptor* was another dinosaur with a

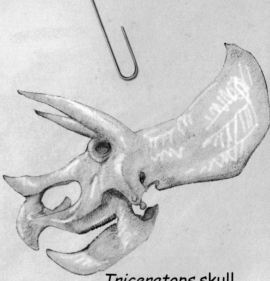

Triceratops skull

beak. It used it to pick up lizards as well as small mammals that looked like mice. *Oviraptor* did not have teeth for chewing. According to paleontologists, though, the muscles that opened and closed its beak allowed the dinosaur to chomp down hard on its food.

Oviraptor skull

I hope that this answers your question, Yasmina!

Professor Brainy

37

Dear Francis,

Tyrannosaurus rex holds the record for the biggest teeth. It had about 50 of them. These were no little teeth, either—they were 6 to 8 inches (15 to 20 cm) long! The name *Tyrannosaurus* means "tyrant reptile." Do you know what a tyrant is? A tyrant is a cruel person who has power over everyone else. And do you know what? It was a perfect name for *Tyrannosaurus*. Its long teeth had very sharp edges and its victims never stood a chance against the dinosaur. The teeth at the front of its jaws were narrower, making them perfect for piercing flesh. *Tyrannosaurus* could then tear off mouthfuls with the help of its powerful jaw muscles.

I've drawn a life-size *Tyrannosaurus* tooth for you. As you can see, it takes up the entire page, which measures 7.5 inches (19 cm) from top to bottom.

Once
Tyrannosaurus
held its prey
between its teeth, the prey
had very little chance to
escape. Brrrr.... the idea
makes me shiver! It seems
that *Tyrannosaurus's* favorite
meal consisted of the duck-billed
herbivores that moved around in herds.

Best wishes,
Professor Brainy

Dear Amanda,

Yes, some plant-eating dinosaurs, the long-necked ones, did indeed swallow stones! I know a paleontologist who has a collection of these stones on display. They are called **gastroliths**. This word comes from Greek, an ancient language that gave us many of our English words.
In "gastrolith," "gastro" means "stomach" and "lith" means "stone." We could actually call them stomach stones!

Gastroliths

41

So, why would
a long-neck
plant-eating dinosaur
swallow stones? *Diplodocus*, a
typical long-neck, had teeth only at
the front of its jaws. It used them
to "rake" leaves, ferns, and fruits.
It swallowed everything without
even chewing!

Once the food reached its stomach,
the grinding process was carried out
by these stones. When the muscles
lining the stomach went into motion,
the stones banged together and
crushed the plants that had been
swallowed. This started up the
digestive process. Bacteria, which
are tiny organisms, completed the

process in the intestine. I should add that *Diplodocus* swallowed these stones at the same time as its meal. They remained stored in its stomach or in its **gizzard**. The gizzard is a pocket located just before the stomach. (Gizzards are also found in birds.)

Once the stones were worn down and too rounded, they passed out of the dinosaur in its droppings. That's why these "stomach stones" are rarely found in the animal's stomach and are more often found elsewhere. Birds today use the same system for eating, except they swallow tiny pebbles that look like gravel.

Your friend,
Professor Brainy

Hi Professor,

We are building a scale model of a prehistoric scene at school. My friends and I would like to know if all dinosaurs were very large. Were there any tiny ones?

Sharise, age 11

Dear Sharise,

Many years ago my sister and I visited Tanzania, a country in Africa. We saw giraffes, lions, and elephants running free in many nature reserves. These animals seemed so big to me. A giraffe stands 19 feet (6 m) tall. That's twice the height of a school bus! An African elephant can weigh 6 tons, which is six times the weight of a car!

As for dinosaurs, they broke the records for size compared to the biggest animals we know today. Some long-necked dinosaurs measured more than 131 feet (40 m) in length, which is twice the length of a city bus. *Brachiosaurus* measured 91 feet (28 m) long and weighed up to 50 tons. That's nine times the weight of an African elephant! *Seismosaurus* measured more than 114 feet (35 m) from the top of its head to the tip of its tail, which made it longer than a tennis court!

To answer your question, though, there were also very small dinosaurs. In fact, there were many more of them. The tiny carnivorous dinosaur called *Sinosauropteryx* measured just 4 feet (1.2 m) long and weighed no more than 22 pounds (10 kg).

Compsognathus was no more than 3 feet (1 m) long and weighed less than 6 pounds (3 kg). It looked a lot more like a chicken than a large dinosaur. So you see, Sharise, not all dinosaurs were giants. Remember this when you are building your scale model!

Have fun!

Professor Brainy

Dear Professor Brainy,
Could there have been herds of dinosaurs the way there are herds of cows today?
Thanks.
Elsa, age 9

Hello Elsa,

That's a very interesting question. Some dinosaurs did live in herds or in packs, just like cows, deer, elephants, and wolves. An entire pack of fossilized small carnivorous dinosaurs was found at Ghost Ranch in New Mexico. Small dinosaurs often hunted in groups to have a better chance of catching prey. What I should make clear, though, is that when paleontologists study dinosaur herds, they mainly use fossilized footprints.

These footprints were preserved because the dinosaurs walked through mud, leaving an imprint of their feet behind. The mud then dried and was quickly covered in sand.

Many imprints were left by a group of long-necked dinosaurs that had once walked on the edge of a river. The biggest footprints are found at the edge of the group and the smallest in the middle. Paleontologists think that the youngest dinosaurs as well as the females stayed in the middle of the herd. They would have been protected by the larger and stronger males, who placed themselves on the outside to watch for danger.

By moving in a herd, the dinosaurs could travel long distances in safety. Other dinosaurs, like the duck-billed species, often lived in herds as well. While some were eating leaves, others kept watch over the area. At any sign of danger, they made noises that could be heard far away by the rest of the group, who could then run. This is how they avoided attacks by large predators. As you can see, these dinosaurs were very well organized!

Regards,
Professor Brainy

How did dinosaurs, with such huge bodies, not get crushed by their own weight?

Thanks, Professor!
Federico, age 12

Hello Federico,

That's a very good point! With some dinosaurs weighing more than 50 tons, it's amazing that the largest of them could even stand on their feet! Let me explain how this was possible by using this illustration.

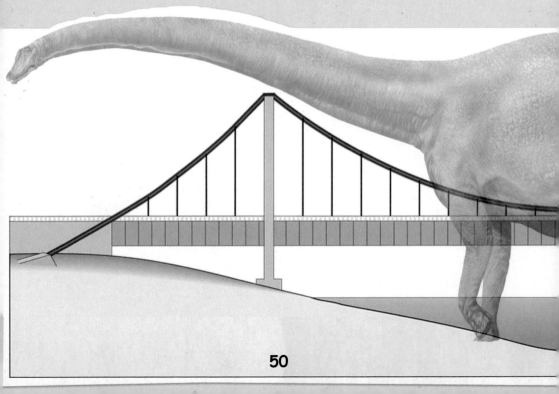

This is a suspension bridge. The road is held up by very thick cables. Why a drawing of a bridge? Well, imagine that one of the largest long-necked dinosaurs, *Diplodocus*, was built something like this bridge.

Its front and back legs are like the bridge's two main pillars. The entire weight of the dinosaur rested on its legs. Its spinal column acted like the cables and held up its huge abdomen.

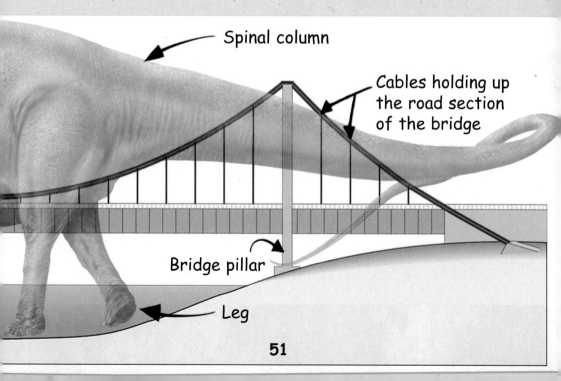

Spinal column

Cables holding up the road section of the bridge

Bridge pillar

Leg

Diplodocus also had rather unusual vertebrae. (Vertebrae are the bones that form small bumps in the middle of your back. They make up the spinal column.) In *Diplodocus*, these bones were doubled up. This made its spinal column much stronger. Thanks to its suspension-bridge skeleton and strong vertebrae, *Diplodocus* could weigh 20 tons and not be crushed under its own weight!

Your friend,
Professor Brainy

Dear Professor Brainy,

Is it true that some dinosaurs were totally covered in armor?

Emilio, age 12

Dear Emilio,

When I was a child, my grandfather often took me to see reenactments of medieval battles. The actors were dressed up like the knights of the Middle Ages. Have you ever seen their armor? It was made to fit perfectly, and covered their body completely. The many plates that made up the armor were joined together and allowed the knight to move. Even so, if he fell to the ground, it was very difficult for him to get up again. Someone usually had to help him. Some herbivorous dinosaurs, such as *Ankylosaurus*, actually had armor that looked like what the medieval knights wore. We call them armored dinosaurs. The bony plates were embedded in their skin. The plates covered them from head to tail, and prevented their enemies from sinking their teeth into them.

Like the knights, these dinosaurs could move about easily because their

Bony plates

Ankylosaurus

54

bony plates were slightly spread apart. Some, like *Euoplocephalus*, had a skull covered in plates. Its eyes were protected by bony eyelids! The animal even had a weapon at the end of its tail—a 66-pound (30 kg) club that it could whip around quickly. But once this dinosaur fell to the ground on its back, that was often the end of it. Its unprotected armorless belly was its weak spot!

Professor Brainy

Club

How did the plant-eating herbivores defend themselves against the ferocious carnivores?

Amin, age 9

Dear Amin,

As I wrote to Emilio, some herbivores were protected by skin of armor. Others had different defense systems. The long-necked *Apatosaurus* had a long tail that it could use like a whip. Mainly, however, it used its height to scare off predators. *Triceratops* had a horn at the end of its nose and another two long horns on its forehead. It used them to defend itself against large carnivores. In addition to the horns, its neck

Head of *Triceratops*

was protected by a wide bony ruff, or collar, that kept its enemies from biting it. Some of the small plant-eating dinosaurs were fast runners, which helped them escape at the first sign of danger.

So, Amin, herbivores had many ways of defending themselves or escaping the jaws of the carnivores!

Take care,
Professor Brainy

Hypsilophodon ran very fast. Its long and powerful legs helped it escape if a carnivorous dinosaur appeared.

Hello Professor!

My family and I just came back from seeing an exhibit on the dinosaurs of the Mesozoic Era. There was a *Stegosaurus* with large plates on its back. What were these plates used for?

Anna, age 10

Dear Anna,

This is a very interesting question. *Stegosaurus* was, as you know already, a "plated dinosaur." It carried two rows of them on its back. The role that these plates played is still a bit of a mystery to scientists. What is almost certain, though, is that they did not help the animal defend itself. Scientists think that they were used to lower or raise the dinosaur's body temperature. How? Well, the plates on *Stegosaurus* were covered in a thin layer of skin lined with many blood vessels. When it was cold, *Stegosaurus* probably turned its plates toward the Sun. The blood running through the vessels in the plates would have warmed up under the Sun's rays, raising the dinosaur's body temperature. If *Stegosaurus* was too hot, on the other hand, it would expose only the thin edges of its plates to the Sun. This would prevent its body temperature from rising further. Amazing, don't you think? There is one more thing I should mention, Anna. Some paleontologists think that the plates on the male stegosaurs changed color to attract females during mating season. What do you and your family think these peculiar plates might have been used for?

Your friend,
Professor Brainy

Stegosaurus

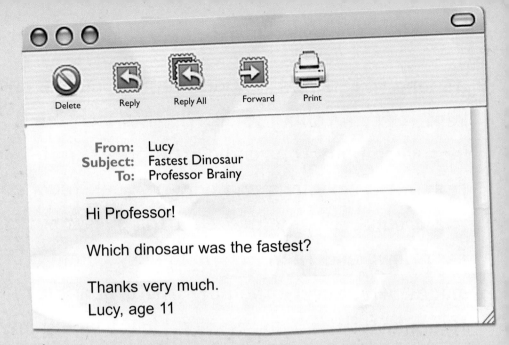

Hi Professor!

Which dinosaur was the fastest?

Thanks very much.
Lucy, age 11

Dear Lucy,

One of the fastest dinosaurs was called *Struthiomimus*, which means "ostrich mimic." Why? Because it looked like today's ostrich, and ran as fast as one, if not faster! If we were to imagine a race between an ostrich, a man, and *Struthiomimus*, the dinosaur would be the winner. It could run about 50 miles per hour (80 km/h), while an ostrich can run only 43 miles per hour (70 km/h). As for the man, he would be left far behind. Even champions in the 100 meter sprint never get above 22 miles per hour (35 km/h)! When *Struthiomimus* ran, its long tail helped to maintain its balance and kept it from falling forward. This dinosaur's legs were built for racing. The bones in its feet were very long and only its toes touched the ground. This helped *Struthiomimus* put its feet down and then lift them very quickly. Its ankles, which were high off the ground, let the animal take long strides. How I would love to climb aboard a time machine and go back to see a *Struthiomimus* race! Would you care to come along, Lucy?

Take care,

Professor Brainy

Hi Professor!

In my books about dinosaurs, the pictures show the same dinosaur with different skin colors. Why is that?

Thank you for your answer.
Camille, age 10

Dear Camille,

That's a very smart question! Scientists can rebuild a dinosaur's skeleton, but reconstructing the skin is a challenge. Do you know why? Well, first of all, skin rarely fossilizes. It decomposes quickly when the dinosaur dies. Paleontologists have, however, found a few skin imprints in rock. Thanks to these traces, they discovered that the skin of dinosaurs was covered in scales, hair, or feathers. But what color were the creatures? That's where the problem lies. The substances that cause coloration, called pigments, are too fragile to withstand the passage of time. Since color does not survive the fossilization process, it is impossible for scientists to know the exact colors of the dinosaurs. They have to use their imagination and become artists. They take their inspiration from the animals of today, like crocodiles, lizards, and birds. Every picture you see of a dinosaur is in some part imaginary. That's why you'll never find a dinosaur with the same colors in every picture!

And so, Camille, if you had to paint the dinosaurs, what colors would you make them?

Your friend,
Professor Brainy

Dear Professor Brainy,

Which dinosaur was the tallest, which one had the longest neck, and which one had the longest tail?

Isaac, age 9

Hi Isaac!

You seem to be fond of records! Before I reveal the names of the winning dinosaurs, there is one thing I should make clear. It is very possible that the names I give you today will change in the future!

As I mentioned earlier, scientists do not know all the dinosaurs that ever existed. There are still many fossils to be dug up and many new species of dinosaurs to be discovered. Who knows, maybe tomorrow paleontologists will come across a species that is even heavier or taller than the ones we know today! And one more thing, Isaac: the formation of a fossil is a very rare phenomenon. It is quite possible that many species of dinosaur were never "captured" in fossil form. Without these traces, it is impossible for us to know about them.

In any case, let's take a look at the dinosaurs that hold records today:

Dinosaur Records:
The tallest: *Sauroposeidon*
59 to 62 feet (18 to 19 m)

The longest: *Seismosaurus*
127 to 147 feet (39 to 45 m)

The heaviest: *Argentinosaurus*
About 100 tons, equal to
20 adult elephants

The longest tail: *Diplodocus*
42 to 45 feet (13 to 14 m)

The longest neck: *Mamenchisaurus*
32 to 45 feet (10 to 14 m)

Best regards,
Professor Brainy

Dear Sofia,

The dinosaurs that carried this odd-looking trumpet on their skull belong to the family of **hadrosaurs**, or duck-billed dinosaurs. The one you are talking about, with the trumpet on its head, is called *Parasaurolophus*. Its hollow crest made out of bone has raised the curiosity of scientists, who have studied it a long time. They have discovered that it was connected to the animal's respiratory, or breathing, system. Air that was inhaled could pass from the mouth to the bony crest and then be let out through the nostrils.

Scientists believe that, using this trumpet, *Parasaurolophus* could send out a powerful sound that could be heard for miles around. Most of these dinosaurs lived in herds, so this loud call would have come in very handy! Imagine the following scene: a large carnivore like *Tyrannosaurus rex* is passing through the area. It spots a herd of *Parasaurolophus*. Hungry for a good meal, *Tyrannosaurus* approaches quietly.

Unfortunately for *Tyrannosaurus*, one of the herd notices it and blows into its "crest-trumpet," warning the others that danger is near.

70

They escape, and *Tyrannosaurus* loses out on dinner! So you see, one of the important roles of this crest was to sound a warning alarm. It may also have been used for other things, like chasing away rivals, attracting females during the mating season, or, simply, communicating. Although I am talking about *Parasaurolophus*, other species of hadrosaur had crests as well. Since all the crests were different, they would have made different kinds of sounds. In this way, every species would have had its own "voice."

Your friend,
Professor Brainy

The air resonated inside the crest, making a sound.

Dear Professor,
My brother Jeremy told
me that dinosaurs laid eggs,
just like chickens. He teases
me a lot, so I would like to
know if this is true.
Simon, age 11

Hello Simon,

Even if Jeremy fools you a lot of the time, he's right about this: dinosaurs did indeed lay eggs, just like chickens and most reptiles today! We call these animals **oviparous**. On the other hand, dinosaur eggs were 2 to 12 times longer than those of chickens! The dinosaur

Dinosaur egg

Chicken egg

eggs and nests that paleontologists have found show us a fascinating side of dinosaur life. Scientists have noted that dinosaurs dug nests and laid anywhere from 10 to 40 eggs, depending on the species. Some of them, like *Oviraptor*, sat on their eggs to hatch them. Most dinosaurs, however, were too heavy. They would have crushed their young. Instead, they covered their nests with sand or leaves, which, as they rotted, would have generated heat and kept the eggs warm. Did you know that even *Tyrannosaurus rex* was a doting parent? It's hard to imagine this ferocious carnivore cuddling its babies, but that was the case!

Tyrannosaurus rex fed its young and kept an eye out for predators looking for easy prey. I think that's sweet, don't you?

Regards,
Professor Brainy

Dinosaur eggs dating from the Cretaceous period

Dear Chloe,

Poor *Oviraptor* has had a bad
reputation as an egg thief
for a long time! Let's take
a closer look at this. In the
early 1920s, the American
Museum of Natural
History in New York City
organized an expedition

to look for fossils in Mongolia, a country in Asia north of China.

Scientists discovered fossils of *Protoceratops* (small-horned dinosaurs), a nest full of dinosaur eggs, and the fossils of another small dinosaur species. The position of this small dinosaur's remains made it seem as though the rascal had died while making a meal out of *Proceratops* eggs! But the story doesn't end there, Chloe. About 70 years later, in 1993, scientists found new *Oviraptor* fossils on top of a nest full of eggs that looked like the ones found in the 1920s.

Inside the eggs, the little dinosaurs had fossilized. Scientists studied these baby dinosaurs, and guess what they found? These eggs really belonged to *Oviraptor*! Far from stealing another dinosaur's eggs, *Oviraptor* had died while protecting its own young. It was quite a surprise to the scientists!

Today, even though the true story has come out, there are still some who believe that *Oviraptor* ate the eggs of other dinosaurs. Now that you know the whole story, you can come to *Oviraptor's* defense!

Best regards,
Professor Brainy

Dear Hugo,

Dinosaurs disappeared at the end of the Cretaceous period, 66 million years ago. And they were not the only ones! Did you know that seven living species out of 10 disappeared at the same time? You can imagine that something terrible must have happened to kill so many animals and plants!

Scientists have tried to figure out what disaster might have occurred. Some believe that a gigantic meteorite, more than 6 miles (10 km) wide, crashed into Earth. A meteorite is a rock that comes from space. Let's try to imagine the event as these scientists see it...

As it crashed to Earth, the meteorite set off huge waves in the ocean and enormous forest fires on land. Many species died, either drowned or trapped by the flames. The impact of the meteorite raised a huge cloud of dust. This dust remained suspended in the air for months, maybe years. Because of it, the Sun's rays could no longer light or heat the planet. You can imagine what a disaster this would be. The first to die were the plants, both on land and in the water. They couldn't survive without sunlight. Next were the herbivorous animals. Without plants to eat, they starved to death. Finally, the carnivorous animals had nothing to eat, and they died, too.

Other scientists think that the eruption of many volcanoes could have spewed a huge amount of toxic gas into the air. Many living species would have died after breathing this poisonous air. Another **theory** suggests that a big drop in temperature on the planet could have killed all species that could not stand the cold. To other scientists, it is a combination of these events (the meteorite, volcanic eruptions, and a drop in temperature) that would have caused many species to disappear at the end of the Cretaceous period.

All these events are possible, Hugo, but evidence gathered by scientists shows that the most likely explanation is that dinosaurs disappeared because of a falling meteorite.

Your friend,
Professor Brainy

Dear Sarah,

I can understand your being frightened. I wouldn't want to find myself face to face with these giant creatures either! Don't worry, though. Scientists are nowhere close to being able to bring dinosaurs back to life. To do this, they would need an essential element called **DNA**. Let me explain what this is. The human body, like all living creatures, is made up of billions of cells. You could compare cells

A section of DNA

to the bricks we use to build our houses. DNA is present in each of our cells. This element is very important because it contains a "blueprint," or instructions, on how the cells should be arranged to create a living creature. For example, the DNA of a dinosaur carries all the information needed to make a new dinosaur. If scientists had this DNA, they could maybe "re-create" one. But they don't have any!

DNA is a fragile substance. The DNA found in the cells that form the bones, teeth, or skin in the fossils we have discovered has not survived the passage of time—in this case, 66 million years! This means, Sarah, that there is very little chance you could ever find yourself face to face with a dinosaur. So have no fear. You can sleep tight tonight!

Warm wishes,
Professor Brainy

Dear Maxime,

That's a good question! As I explained to Hugo on page 79, all the dinosaurs disappeared during a disaster that occurred in the Cretaceous period. Other species, however, managed to survive. Some of these species were descendants, or relatives, of the dinosaurs!

What animal today could be related to the dinosaurs? Let me give you a hint. If you want to meet a descendant of a dinosaur, all you have to do is look up at the sky. Yes, you guessed right! Scientists believe that the descendants of the dinosaurs are the birds! How did they come up with this idea?

In 1860, some men working in a **quarry** in Germany discovered the imprint of a feather that dated back 150 million years. Scientists gave the feather's owner the name *Archaeopteryx*, which means "ancient wing."

A year later, a complete skeleton, surrounded by feathers identical to the one that had been found, was discovered in the same place. The skeleton of this strange animal looked a lot like a dinosaur. It had a bony tail, clawed fingers, pointed teeth, and long hind legs. But that's not all! Besides being covered in feathers, it had front legs shaped like wings.

Archaeopteryx fossil

This led scientists to believe that *Archaeopteryx* could have fluttered from tree to tree to catch flying insects. This was a fantastic discovery, Maxime! It showed us that the first "bird" was indeed a dinosaur!

Recent discoveries in China support this theory. Scientists have discovered the imprint of feathers on many fossilized skeletons of carnivorous dinosaurs. Our birds today no longer resemble dinosaurs, of course. But it's easy to believe that they are the descendants of this first flying dinosaur! I'm sure that Granddad *Archaeopteryx* would be proud to see his offspring today!

Regards,
Professor Brainy

Archaeopteryx

Dear Professor,
My sister and I would really like to find some dinosaur fossils. Where is a good place to look for them? Also, could you tell us where scientists have found the most dinosaur fossils?
Thanks a lot.
Charlotte and Lea, ages 10 and 12

Dear Charlotte and Lea,

I see we have two budding detectives here! This reminds me of the vacations I spent with my sister when we were children. We used to have fun finding as many fossils as we could. We searched everywhere. I must admit that my sister usually beat me at this game because she had a sharp eye! But they weren't really dinosaur fossils we were digging up, they were seashells. Finding

Seashell fossil

dinosaur fossils today is far from easy! Before going off on an adventure, scientists spend hundreds of hours searching through books to figure out what areas are most likely to "collect" fossils. They also check to see if these areas have rock that is between 230 and 66 million years old (remember, that's the period in which the dinosaurs lived). Once they have this data, they can organize an expedition and leave with their team.

Sites where the most dinosaur fossils have been found include Dinosaur Provincial Park in Alberta, Canada, and the Douglass Quarry in Jensen, Utah. Other parts of North America, as well as South America (Argentina), Asia

(China, Mongolia), Africa (Tanzania), and Australia are also home to some of the best fossil sites. Still, plenty of regions remain unexplored. I'm certain the future holds many surprises. Who knows, maybe one day you'll take part in an expedition and discover a new species of dinosaur!

Your friend,
Professor Brainy

Dear Professor Brainy,

When were the very first dinosaur fossils found?

Peter, age 9

Dear Peter,

I am sure that people of every era have stumbled across dinosaur fossils. Our distant ancestors, however, would have had no idea that dinosaurs ever existed. That's perfectly understandable. Scientists have only been studying fossils for 200 years. Our scientific knowledge has come a long way during this time. We now have a much better understanding of the history of life on Earth. The very first dinosaur fossils were identified a little more than 160 years ago. Here is how it happened: between 1818 and 1824, British scientist William Buckland analyzed the fossilized bones of a gigantic reptile. He called it *Megalosaurus*, which means "giant lizard."

At the same time, another British scientist, Dr. Gideon Mantell, made an interesting discovery. He found some large teeth embedded in stone. He saw they looked a lot like iguana teeth, but were much larger. He thought they were from a giant iguana. Mantell gave their owner the name *Iguanodon*, which means "reptile with iguana teeth."

An iguana is a large lizard that lives in Central and South America. The longest specimens may measure more than 6 feet (2 m) in length, including the tail.

In 1842, while studying giant fossils discovered in England, British paleontologist Richard Owen realized that the reptiles that were found were very different from any he had known. They were much taller, and much bigger. He decided to classify them in a separate family that he named "dinosaur." The word "dinosaur" comes from Greek, an ancient language that has given us many of the words we use today. "Dino" comes from *deinos*, which means "terrible," and "saur" comes from *sauros*, which means "reptile." Owen wasn't the first to find dinosaur fossils, but he was certainly the first to identify these "terrible lizards."

Regards,
Professor Brainy

Delete

Reply

Reply All

Forward

Print

From: Noah
Subject: Where to see dinosaur fossils
To: Professor Brainy

```
Dear Professor,

Where can I go to see

dinosaur skeletons?

Noah, age 8
```

Hello Noah,

There are complete dinosaur skeletons on display in museums all over the world!
I am attaching a list of the biggest museums that exhibit these impressive creatures.

Where to See Dinosaur Fossils

Museum of Natural History
    Paris, France
Museum of Natural History
    London, England
Museum of Natural History
    Berlin, Germany
American Museum of Natural History
    New York, United States
Royal Tyrrell Museum
    Drumheller, Alberta, Canada
Zigong Dinosaur Museum
    Zigong, Sichuan Province, China
Queensland Museum
    Brisbane, Queensland, Australia

The skeletons you will find in these museums have been reconstructed. It is rare to find complete fossilized dinosaur skeletons.
The bones of a dinosaur skeleton are often scattered before the body has a chance to

fossilize. Other animals walking by may trample the bones, or river currents may wash them away. This explains why fossil hunters often find nothing more than a partial skeleton. Most of the time, they only dig up a few separate bones or a handful of teeth. These bits of skeleton are often displayed behind windows, along with gastroliths (the stones that dinosaurs swallowed to help them digest), **coprolites** (fossilized droppings), and the imprints of feet and skin.

Have fun on your next visit to one of these museums!

Your friend,
Professor Brainy

Glossary

carnivore animal that eats meat

coniferous type of trees or shrubs that bear cones and evergreen leaves

coprolites fossilized dung

Cretaceous the geological period spanning from roughly 145 million to 66 million years ago; the third period of the Mesozoic era

dinosaur a member of an extinct race of reptiles of the Mesozoic era, belonging to the group Dinosauria

DNA the abbreviation for deoxyribonucleic acid, a double-stranded molecule that contains the genetic instructions to all life forms

fossil the preserved remains of a plant or animal from a past geologic age

Glossary

gastrolith a stone swallowed by an animal to aid with digestion

gizzard a thick muscular sac located near the stomach of birds and dinosaurs used to grind and digest food

hadrosaur a duck-billed dinosaur

herbivore animal that feeds only on plants

Jurassic the geological period spanning from roughly 200 million to 145 million years ago; the second period of the Mesozoic era

Mesozoic an era of geological time when dinosaurs existed, spanning the periods between 250 million and 66 million years ago

mollusk an invertebrate (spineless) animal, such as a snail, with a soft unsegmented body and usually protected by a shell

Glossary

omnivore animal that feeds on both plants and animals

Ornithischians branch of dinosaur with a pelvic structure similar to that of lizards; only herbivores fall in this branch

oviparous able to lay eggs, like birds, reptiles, and dinosaurs

paleontologist a person who studies prehistoric life by examining plant and animal fossils

Pangaea the single giant continent of the Paleozoic and Mesozoic eras, which later separated to form the existing continents

prehistoric belonging to, or relating to, the period of time before the first accounts of people or recorded history

Glossary

quarry a site where stone, fossils or other materials are extracted by digging or blasting

Saurischians branch of dinosaur with a pelvic structure similar to that of birds; includes both carnivores and herbivores

sedimentary rock a type of rock formed by compaction of sediment, including the remains of plants, animals and rock fragments

species a class of things of the same kind and with the same name

theory a general rule offered to explain experiences or facts

Triassic the geological period spanning from roughly 250 million to 200 million years ago; the first period of the Mesozoic era

⚬~ For More Information ~⚬

Dinosaur Encyclopedia. Jayne Parsons (editor) (DK Publishing, Inc., New York, 2001)

National Geographic Dinosaurs. Paul Barrett, Raul Martin (illustrator), Kevin Padian (National Geographic Children's Books, 2001)

Bones Rock!: Everything You Need to Know to Be a Paleontologist. Peter Larson and Kristin Donnan (Invisible Cities Press, 2004)

National Audubon Society Field Guide to North American Fossils. Ida Thompson (Knopf, New York, 2000)

Coop's Map Guide to Dinosaur Sites and Museums. Coop's Maps (Lone Mountain Design, 1999)

The Random House Dinosaur Travel Guide. Kelly Milner Halls (Random House, 2006)

For More Information

Web sites:

Encyclopaedia Britannica: Discovering Dinosaurs
http://www.britannica.com/dinosaurs/dinosaurs/index2.html

National Geographic Prehistoric World
http://science.nationalgeographic.com/science/prehistoric-world.html

PBS Evolution: What Killed the Dinosaurs?
http://www.pbs.org/wgbh/evolution/extinction/dinosaurs

Smithsonian National Museum of Natural History: The Department of Paleobiology
http://paleobiology.si.edu

University of California Museum of Paleontology: Student Resources
http://www.ucmp.berkeley.edu/education/students.php

~ Index ~

～ Index ～